MEDITATIC ⸻

MINDFULNESS:

The Power Of The
Present Moment

*Take Control of Yourself, Your
Thoughts and Emotions, Reduce
Stress, Anxiety and Improve
Concentration*

__By Yumi Tanaka__

3

INTRODUCTION

WHAT IS MEDITATION AND MINDFULNESS

Meditation is an ancient practice that has roots in the spiritual traditions of many cultures. It has been practiced for centuries to achieve inner peace and self-awareness. In a world that is now fast-paced and stressful, meditation is becoming increasingly popular as a way to relieve tension and improve mental and physical health. Mindfulness, which is a form of meditation based on present-moment awareness, is increasingly accepted in the medical community as a way to treat disorders such as anxiety, depression and insomnia.

This book will explore the world of meditation and mindfulness, providing information on their origins as well as their potential benefits on health and well-being. The book will also address how meditation and mindfulness can be incorporated into daily life to improve concentration, reduce stress and tension, and achieve greater inner peace. With practical examples and suggestions for getting started on your meditation path, this reading will give you the knowledge and tools you need to best learn how to reap the benefits of meditation and mindfulness.

In addition, a more general section about practical tips for improving one's physical well-being will also be covered. The book will include suggestions for a more balanced and mindful lifestyle, including a healthy diet, regular exercise, and time management. You will be given concrete examples of how to integrate these elements into your daily life to achieve the best results for your physical and mental health.

In summary, this handbook is a comprehensive guide to making the most of the potential of meditation and mindfulness to improve your life. Whether you are a beginner or an expert in meditation, this book will provide you with the tools you need to achieve greater inner peace and a more balanced and happy life.

HISTORICAL BACKGROUND OF MEDITATION AND MINDFULNESS

Meditation has centuries-old origins dating back more than 5,000 years in ancient India and Tibet. Meditation was considered an integral part of the spiritual and philosophical practices of these cultures and was used to achieve inner peace and greater self-awareness. Meditation was later imported to China with Buddhism, where it was further developed and spread.

Mindfulness, which is a form of meditation based on present-moment awareness, has its roots in Buddhism and East Asian spiritual traditions. The practice was introduced to the United States in 1970 when Jon Kabat-Zinn developed a meditation-based mindfulness program called MBSR (Mindfulness-Based Stress Reduction). Later, MBSR was also used to treat medical conditions such as anxiety, depression, and chronic pain.

Through the centuries, meditation and mindfulness have been imported to Europe and other parts of the world through the spread of Buddhism and Asian spiritual traditions. In recent decades, these practices have become increasingly popular around the world as a way to improve quality of life. In addition, to date they have been positively evaluated for their effectiveness in treating mental and physical conditions.

THE SCIENCE OF MEDITATION, HOW IT AFFECTS THE BRAIN AND BODY, THE BENEFITS OF MEDITATION ON THE MIND AND BODY

The science behind meditation is very fascinating and involves both physiology and neuroscience. Much research has been done in recent years to study the effect of meditation and mindfulness on the brain and body by examining how these practices affect the cognitive, emotional, and physical functions of the human body.

One of the first discoveries in science was that meditation can increase gray matter density in areas of the brain associated with memory, learning, attention and emotional regulation. This means that this activity can help strengthen these brain areas, increasing their ability to function and resist potential injury. A study conducted on a group of people who practiced meditation for more than eight weeks also found increased production of brain cells in the prefrontal cortex, a region of the brain responsible for self-control. These phenomena are effective in reducing symptoms of anxiety and depression and increased resilience to stress.

In addition, meditation has been associated with decreased activity in the amygdala, an area of the brain responsible for regulating fear and anxiety. Meditation can affect our brains by decreasing the activity of the sympathetic nervous system, which is responsible for the "fight or flight" response to danger, and increasing the activity of the parasympathetic nervous system, which is responsible for the "relax and regenerate" response.

Practicing this activity also has positive consequences in terms of reducing chronic inflammation, which is associated with many cardiovascular diseases and diabetes. Other studies have shown that meditation can have positive effects on blood pressure, the immune system, and sleep quality, and may be associated with a reduction in the frequency and intensity of pain, both acute and chronic.

Other scientific studies have shown that the regular practice of meditation and mindfulness can improve memory, concentration and decision-making ability. In fact, these activities can help reduce procrastination and mental distraction, which in turn can help develop a greater capacity for attention and concentration, both in daily life and in work or study by increasing productivity.
Benefits have been demonstrated in the treatment of many health conditions, including anxiety, depression, insomnia, attention-deficit hyperactivity disorder (ADHD) and addictions. In many studies there have been similar or even better results than conventional pharmacological or psychological treatments for these conditions.

In conclusion, meditation acts on the brain and body through modulation of the stress response. During meditation, levels of cortisol, the stress hormone, are reduced, while levels of oxytocin, the feel-good hormone, increase. These changes in hormone levels affect the body's stress response and nervous system response, helping to manage emotions and consequently improve mental and physical health

Indeed, with regular practice, meditation and mindfulness can help create a balance between body and mind and improve quality of life and mental and physical well-being. In summary, the science behind meditation is very interesting and involves both physiology and neuroscience. Studies on meditation have shown that regular practice of this technique can have positive effects on physical and mental health.

For example, a study conducted on a group of people who practiced meditation for more than eight weeks found an increase in gray matter density in the prefrontal cortex, a region of the brain that is responsible for emotion regulation, attention and self-control. This increase in gray matter was associated with reduced symptoms of anxiety and depression and increased resilience to stress.

Other studies have shown that meditation can have positive effects on blood pressure, the immune system, and sleep quality. In addition, meditation has been associated with a reduction in the frequency and intensity of pain, both acute and chronic.

Meditation acts on the brain and body through modulation of the stress response. During meditation, levels of cortisol, the stress hormone, are reduced, while levels of oxytocin, the feel-good hormone, increase. These changes in hormone levels affect the body's stress response and nervous system response, helping to reduce anxiety and stress and improve mental and physical health.

In conclusion, the science behind meditation and mindfulness supports the claim that these practices can help improve physical and mental health. Studies suggest that meditation and mindfulness can positively affect the brain, immune system, blood pressure and sleep quality, as well as reduce anxiety, stress and pain. With regular practice, meditation and mindfulness can help create a balance between body and mind and improve quality of life.

WHY LEARNING TO MANAGE OUR EMOTIONS IS CRUCIAL TO ACHIEVING MENTAL WELL-BEING AND HAPPINESS

Sometimes, emotions can be overwhelming, so learning to manage them is crucial to achieving mental well-being and happiness. When we fail to control them these can negatively affect our daily lives and our relationships with others especially if they are anger and sadness.

For example, if we are overwhelmed by negative emotions, we may have impulsive or emotional reactions, which can cause problems with people we love or with our work performance. In addition, a lack of control in some situations can increase stress and anxiety, which in turn can lead to physical and mental health problems.

On the other hand, when we are able to manage our emotions, we are able to live more balanced and fulfilling lives: we can make more reasonable decisions, face life's challenges with greater resilience, and not be overwhelmed by emotionality. All this helps to maintain healthy and positive relationships with others, which in

18

turn can contribute to our mental well-being and happiness.

In summary, learning to manage our emotions is crucial to living more peacefully and satisfactorily. Meditation and mindfulness are powerful tools that help us achieve this by increasing awareness of our emotions and helping us manage them more productively.

WHY FOCUSING ON THE PRESENT IS THE BEST WAY TO ENJOY LIFE

Focusing on the present moment is an essential approach to living a happy and fulfilling life. We often tend to project too much into the past or future, without considering the present. We think about the things we have done in the past, brooding over our mistakes and what we have been denied, or we worry excessively about what our life may be like later. This attitude prevents us from living up to our full potential and makes us miss the opportunity to enjoy every moment.

Why is focusing on the present moment the best way to live life? Because it is the only thing we really have control over. We cannot control the past, but we can learn from it. We cannot control the future, but we can plan and prepare for it.

Living fully in the present allows us to experience life more consciously and appreciate each moment. It allows us to be present and take care of our needs, desires and dreams. It helps us reduce stress and anxiety and improve concentration. It also allows us to connect with others and build healthy, lasting relationships.

Ultimately, focusing on the present moment can be a practice that takes time, practice and effort however once we become more aware and begin to have the first results, life becomes more meaningful and more fulfilling. All of this helps us to be more rewarding and strong in facing challenges, become more mindful, and stress less about things that are not about the moment we are living in. Only in this way can we appreciate life to its fullest potential by connecting with others in the best way possible.

UNDERSTAND HOW THE MIND WORKS, HOW OUR THOUGHTS AND EMOTIONS AFFECT OUR MOOD AND OUR DAILY ROUTINE

The human mind is a complex entity that is divided into two distinct sections, the rational area and the emotional area. The rational area is responsible for logic, decisions and planning, while the emotional area handles emotions, instinctive reactions and emotional responses. These two areas work together to form an individual's personality and significantly affect his or her daily life.

Thoughts and emotions have a profound impact on our mood and emotional stability. They can determine our ability to relate to others, to love and be loved, and to cope with life in a balanced way. However, negative thoughts and destructive emotions can negatively affect our physical and psychological well-being, leading to mental and physical health problems.

Although the rational sphere is important for planning and decision-making, we should not underestimate the importance of the emotional sphere. Happiness, inner peace, and personal satisfaction come from the ability to manage and regulate one's emotions, to understand them, and to express them to the best of one's ability.

In conclusion, understanding the nature of the mind and how it works is fundamental to making the rational and emotional spheres work together in a healthy way. Meditation and mindfulness are effective tools to help achieve this balance, enabling us to become aware of our emotions and thoughts and manage them more effectively, improving the quality of our lives and increasing inner peace and happiness.

TOWARD A MINDFUL MEDITATION

THE FIRST STEPS TOWARD MEDITATION: HOW TO APPROACH MEDITATION PRACTICE

The basic first step in approaching meditation is to find a quiet, comfortable place where we can sit in silence and without distraction. This place can actually be anywhere where we feel in suitable peace of mind that we can relax and be able to spend time with ourselves, from the comfort of a bed to the stillness of a park. It is important to choose a place where you feel comfortable, so that you can relax and focus on your meditative practice to the best of your ability.

The second thing to do is to choose the right meditation technique. There are many different techniques, each with its own specific goal and degree of difficulty. For example, transcendental meditation, mindfulness meditation and Vipassana meditation are just some of the most popular techniques. Each of these techniques requires a different level of commitment and focus on specific aspects of meditation, such as concentration and mindfulness.

To succeed in meditative practice, it is also important to be open to different techniques and schools of thought. There are many ways to achieve the same goals in meditation, and it is often necessary to experiment with several of them before finding the one that best suits one's needs and preferences. Also, be aware that meditation is a personal experience, and what works for one person may not work for another. If you are new to meditation, it is recommended to start with a simple meditation technique, such as mindfulness meditation. This technique focuses on being present in the present moment, without judging or worrying about the past or future. You can practice mindfulness simply by focusing your attention on your breathing or the sounds you hear around you, or by doing guided visualization to relax and empty your mind.

The third step is to establish a daily meditation routine. Even if you meditate for only a few minutes a day, regularity is key to gaining the benefits of the practice. It is important to choose a time of day when you can set aside time, such as in the morning before you start your day or in the evening before you go to sleep. In addition, it is crucial to find a way to maintain consistency in practice, such as setting a reminder on your phone or marking practice in a personal journal.

Finally, another important factor in meditation practice is consistency. It is not enough to meditate once a week or only during particularly stressful situations. Meditation requires constant and regular practice to achieve maximum benefits. With this in mind, it is helpful to set a daily or weekly goal for the duration of the practice in order to maintain a consistent focus. Meditation should not be viewed as an activity isolated from daily life, but an opportunity to develop greater awareness and a more positive approach to life.

The fourth step is to understand the importance of having an open mind and willing to learn is crucial to meditation practice. Often you may encounter obstacles during meditation, such as having difficulty concentrating or keeping up the required amount of time, or you may feel frustration at not getting results right away or solving all the problems of stress, anxiety or concentration. In such cases, it is important to have an attitude of acceptance and patience. Only through open-mindedness and a willingness to learn can one progress in practice while reaping maximum benefits. It takes commitment and patience, but also a constant willingness to improve oneself. It is important to remember that it is not an immediate solution to life's problems, but rather a path that takes time and dedication, but will bring excellent and lasting results in the long run.

The fifth piece of advice is not to judge one's meditation practice. Often, beginners judge themselves harshly when they encounter difficulties in their practice, but it is important to remember that meditation is a personal path that is not always easy. Instead of judging yourself, you should accept your thoughts and feelings during practice and focus on breathing and present-moment awareness.

Finally, another important tip is to seek support and guidance if needed. There are many online or in-person meditation groups, and they can often be helpful in getting support and suggestions during practice. In case of difficulty, it is advisable to consult an experienced meditation teacher for further advice and guidance on which meditation technique to apply.

In conclusion, taking the first steps in meditation practice requires commitment and perseverance, but also an attitude of open-mindedness and willingness to learn. With time and regular practice, one can make great progress in one's meditation practice.
All this can bring great benefits to the mind and body, improving the quality of life and increasing mental and physical well-being.

In the following sections we will go on to present the various existing meditation techniques step-by-step, starting with the simplest and most accessible techniques and gradually increasing in complexity and difficulty. In this way, anyone who wants to start practicing meditation will have a clear, step-by-step path to follow, and will be able to choose the meditation technique that best suits their needs and abilities.

MINDFULNESS MEDITATION

Mindfulness meditation is one of the most popular and accessible meditation techniques. Mindfulness meditation focuses on being present in the present moment, without judging or worrying about the past or future. In this way, mindfulness meditation can help reduce stress, improve concentration and increase awareness. Here is how to practice mindfulness meditation step-by-step:

1.   Choose a quiet place where you can sit or lie down comfortably. Make sure the place is distraction-free and quiet.

2.   Find a comfortable position that allows you to be relaxed but alert. You can sit in a chair or on a meditation pillow, or lie on a yoga mat.

3.   Focus on your breathing. Focus on the air going in and out of your nose, on the sensation

of your chest expanding and contracting with each breath. If your mind wanders, refocus on your breathing.

4. During mindfulness meditation, your thoughts may wander: observe them without judging them or reacting to them. Let thoughts pass by like clouds in the sky, without getting caught up in them.

5. Listen to the sensations in your body. Feel the sensation of your back against the pillow, the contact of your hands with your legs, the breath flowing through your body.

6. During mindfulness meditation, the goal is to be present in the moment. Be aware of what is happening in the present moment, without worrying about the past or future.

7. Practice meditation regularly: mindfulness meditation requires regularity to produce lasting results. Try to practice meditation every day, even for just a few minutes, to achieve maximum benefici.

Mindfulness meditation can be practiced anywhere, at any time of the day. You can do a short mindfulness meditation in the morning to prepare for the day, or a mindfulness meditation in the evening to relax your mind before bed. Mindfulness meditation is a very flexible activity and can be customized to suit your needs and preferences.

In summary, mindfulness meditation is a simple and effective meditation technique that focuses on being present in the present moment, without judging or worrying about the past or future.

"GUIDED" MEDITATION

Guided meditation is a meditation technique that relies on guided visualization and imagination. Instead of focusing on breathing or body sensations, as in mindfulness meditation, guided meditation takes you on an imaginary journey that can help you relax your mind and body, reduce stress and anxiety, and improve overall well-being.

Here's how to practice guided meditation step-by-step:

1. Choose a quiet place: as with most meditation techniques, it is important to choose a quiet place where you can sit or lie comfortably without distractions or noise.

2. Choose an image or phrase: For guided meditation, choose an image or phrase that helps you relax and focus. You might imagine yourself on a quiet beach, or repeat a phrase such as "I am calm and quiet".

3.   Follow the instructions: start following the instructions of the guided meditation. You might listen to an audio recording of the guided meditation, or have a teacher guide you through the meditation. Follow the instructions and let your imagination guide you. I provide below an example of instructions for the journey, but for this type of meditation I recommend listening to the instructions, there not numerous free videos you can draw from, for example on You Tube.

Sample journey instructions:
•   Choose an image or phrase: For this guided meditation, choose an image or phrase that helps you relax and focus. You might imagine yourself on a quiet beach, or repeat a phrase such as "I am calm and quiet".

•   Begin the meditation: close your eyes and start breathing deeply. Focus on your breathing, and observe how air enters and leaves your nose.

• Picture the image or repeat the sentence: begin by picturing the image you have chosen, or repeat the sentence you have chosen to focus. Visualize yourself in a situation of peace and calmness, or repeat the sentence slowly and intentionally.

• Visualize your breath: keep breathing deeply, and visualize your breath as a wave of energy going in and out of your body.

• Relax and let go: let guided meditation bring you into a state of deep relaxation. Let go of all worries and thoughts, and focus only on the image or phrase you have chosen.

• Finish the meditation: when you are ready, slowly open your eyes and take a moment to notice how you feel. Breathe deeply and let the feeling of calm and serenity accompany you for the rest of the day.

4.	Observe your sensations: during guided meditation, observe the sensations in your body and mind. You can notice how you feel, both physically and emotionally. Let the sensations pass without judging them or reacting to them.

5.	Practice meditation regularly: as with all meditation techniques, guided meditation requires regular practice to produce lasting results. Try to practice guided meditation every day, even for just a few minutes, for maximum benefits.

Guided meditation is a very flexible activity and can be tailored to one's needs and preferences. There are many audio recordings of guided meditations available online, both free and paid, covering a wide range of themes and goals. You can also create your own guided meditation, choosing the images or phrases that best suit your needs.

In summary, guided meditation is a meditation technique that relies on guided visualization and imagination. Guided meditation can be practiced anywhere, at any time of the day, and is a very flexible activity that can be customized to suit your needs and preferences.

WALKING MEDITATION

Walking meditation is a form of active meditation that uses the movement of walking to help focus and relax. Walking meditation is a very accessible meditation technique that can be practiced anywhere there is an open space in which to walk.
Here is how to practice walking meditation step-by-step:

1. Choose a quiet place: choose a quiet place where you can walk without distractions or noise. An outdoor place, such as a park or beach, is ideal for walking meditation.

2. Choose a walking pace: choose a walking pace that allows you to walk smoothly and steadily. There is no need to walk too fast, but try to maintain a steady pace.

3.   Focus on the sensation of walking: during walking meditation, focus on the sensation of walking. Focus on the sensation of feet rising and falling, the sensation of breath flowing through the body, and the sensation of wind on the skin.

4.   Observe the surrounding nature: during walking meditation, observe the surrounding nature. Observe the trees, flowers, birds and animals. Let the beauty of nature help you relax and concentrate.

5.   Observe your mind: during walking meditation, observe your mind and thoughts. Let the thoughts pass by like clouds in the sky, without judging them or reacting to them. Be present in the present moment, and allow the mind to relax.

6.   Practice meditation regularly: as with all meditation techniques, walking meditation requires regular practice to produce lasting

results. Try to practice walking meditation every day, even for just a few minutes, for maximum benefits.

Walking meditation is a very flexible activity that is also customizable. You can practice walking meditation anywhere there is an open space in which to walk, and it can be a good alternative to sitting meditation for those who have difficulty sitting still for long periods.
Walking meditation is a form of active meditation that uses the movement of walking to help you focus and relax. Walking meditation is a very accessible meditation technique that can be practiced anywhere there is an open space in which to walk. Walking meditation can help reduce stress, improve concentration and increase awareness, and can be customized to suit your needs and preferences.It is a very simple meditation technique, but can be very powerful if practiced regularly.

Here are some suggestions for improving your walking meditation practice:

• Start slowly: If you are new to walking meditation, start slowly. Try to walk for 10 to 15 minutes a day, and then gradually increase the duration of your practice.

• Focus on the sensation of walking: walking meditation is based on the sensation of walking, so try to focus on this sensation. Observe how the feet rise and fall, and how the breath flows through the body.

• Keep a steady pace: try to maintain a steady pace during your walking meditation. There is no need to walk too fast, but try to maintain a steady pace.

• Be present in the moment: during your walking meditation, be present in the present moment. Let your mind relax and observe the surrounding nature.

• Practice meditation regularly: as with all meditation techniques, walking meditation requires regular practice to produce lasting results. Try to practice walking meditation every day, even for just a few minutes, for maximum benefits.

Walking meditation can be a good alternative to sitting meditation for those who have difficulty sitting still for long periods of time.

FOCUS MEDITATION

Focus meditation is a meditation technique that relies on concentrating on a specific object or sound, such as breathing or a repeated word. Focus meditation can help reduce stress, improve concentration and increase awareness. Here is how to practice concentrative meditation step-by-step:

• Choose a quiet place: choose a quiet place where you can sit comfortably without distractions or noises.

• Choose an object of concentration: choose an object of concentration to focus on. You can choose your breathing, a repeated word or sound, or anything else that helps you focus.

• Sit comfortably: sit comfortably with your back straight and your hands resting on your knees.

• Focus on the object of concentration: start by focusing on the object of concentration you have chosen. If you have chosen breathing, focus your attention on inhaling and exhaling. If you have chosen a repeated word or sound, repeat it slowly and intentionally.

• Observe your mind: during concentrative meditation, observe your mind and thoughts. Let thoughts pass by like clouds in the sky, without judging them or reacting to them.

• Go back to the focus object: when the mind gets distracted, return to the focus object you have chosen. No matter how many times the mind gets distracted, it keeps returning to the focus object.

• Practice meditation regularly: as with all meditation techniques, focus meditation requires regular practice to produce lasting results. Try to practice concentrative focus meditation every day, even for just a few minutes, for maximum benefits.

Focus meditation can be adapted to you as you see fit. You can choose the focus object that best suits your needs, and you can use focus meditation to achieve different goals, such as reducing stress, increasing concentration, or improving general well-being.

In summary, focus meditation is a meditation technique that relies on focusing on a specific object or sound. Focus meditation can help reduce stress, improve concentration and increase awareness.

YOGA

Yoga is an ancient practice that combines exercise, breathing, and meditation to improve overall health and well-being. Yoga is a very flexible practice and can be tailored to individual needs and preferences. I will now provide you with very general steps for practicing yoga as the complete practice would require a whole separate book.

Here is how to practice yoga step-by-step:

1.   Choose a quiet place: choose a quiet place where you can practice yoga without distractions or noises.

2.   Choose a type of yoga: there are many types of yoga to choose from, such as Hatha yoga, Ashtanga yoga, Kundalini yoga, and many others. Choose the type of yoga that best suits your needs and preferences.

3. Choose yoga equipment: to practice yoga, you will need good equipment, such as a yoga mat, yoga block, and yoga strap.

4. Sit in meditation position: begin your yoga practice by sitting in meditation position with your back straight and your hands resting on your knees. Close your eyes and start breathing deeply.

5. Practice yoga postures: begin performing the yoga postures you have chosen for your practice. Observe how you feel as you perform the postures, and focus your attention on the breath.

6. Practice meditation: after performing the yoga postures, practice meditation to relax and focus. Close your eyes and start breathing deeply, focusing on the sensation of the breath flowing through your body.

7.   Finish your practice: when you are ready, slowly open your eyes and take a moment to notice how you feel. Breathe deeply and let the feeling of calm and serenity accompany you for the rest of the day.

Yoga is a very flexible practice and can be customized to suit your needs and preferences. You can choose the type of yoga that best suits your needs, and you can use yoga to achieve different goals, such as reducing stress, improving flexibility, or enhancing general well-being.

In summary, yoga is an ancient practice that combines movement, breathing, and meditation to improve health and overall well-being.

METTA MEDITATION

Metta meditation, also known as loving kindness meditation, is a Buddhist meditation practice that focuses on cultivating thoughts of loving kindness toward oneself and others. Metta meditation can help reduce stress, improve relationship with self and others, and increase mindfulness.

Metta meditation can be customized according to one's needs and preferences. Many practitioners prefer to begin the practice of Metta Meditation by addressing love and kindness first to themselves and their loved ones, and then gradually expand the circle of people to whom they address love and kindness. Here is how to practice Metta Meditation step-by-step:

1.   Choose a quiet place: choose a quiet place where you can sit comfortably without distractions or noise.

2.   Sit comfortably: sit comfortably with your back straight and your hands resting on your lap.

3.   Breathe deeply: start breathing deeply and focus on the sensation of the breath flowing through your body.

4.   Address love to yourself: imagine a version of yourself in front of you and send thoughts of loving kindness toward yourself. Repeat phrases such as "May I be happy and free from pain" or "May I be at peace and serene."

5.   Address love to loved ones: think of the people dearest to you and send thoughts of loving kindness toward them. Repeat phrases such as "May my mother/father/brother/sister be happy and free from sorrow" or "May my best friend/friend be at peace and serene."

6.   Address love to neutral people: think of people you don't know very well or rarely meet, and send thoughts of loving kindness toward them. Repeat phrases such as "May my neighbor be happy and free from pain" or "May the supermarket clerk be at peace and serene."

7.   Address love to difficult people: finally, think about the people you have difficulty relating to and send thoughts of loving kindness toward them. Repeat phrases such as "May the person who hurt me be happy and free from pain" or "May my boss be at peace and serene." This step is definitely the most difficult as it involves wishing good to the people who have hurt us. However, only by overcoming hatred, through forgiveness, love and compassion can we truly achieve inner peace and true happiness.

8.   Cultivate thoughts of loving kindness toward all living beings: finally, imagine that you have before you all living beings in the world, and send thoughts of love and kindness toward

them. Repeat phrases such as "May all living beings be happy and free from pain" or "May all living beings be at peace and serene."

9.   Practice meditation regularly: as with all meditation techniques, Metta meditation requires regular practice to produce lasting results. Try to practice Metta meditation every day, even for just a few minutes, for maximum benefits.

Metta meditation is a simple but powerful meditation practice that can help foster positive thoughts of love and compassion toward self and others, resulting in improved mood and perception of the world around us. Metta meditation can be customized to one's needs and preferences, and can be used to achieve various goals, such as reducing stress, improving relationships with yourself and others, and increasing mindfulness.

SHAMBALA MEDITATION

Shambala meditation is a meditation technique that has its roots in the Tibetan Buddhist tradition. This practice focuses on creating an inner environment of peace and calmness where a person can relax and focus.

Here is how to practice Shambala meditation step-by-step:

1.   Choose a quiet place: choose a quiet place where you can sit comfortably without distractions or noise.

2.   Sit comfortably: sit comfortably with your back straight and your hands resting on your lap.

3.   Breathe deeply: start breathing deeply and focus on the sensation of the breath flowing through your body.

4.   Visualize a sphere of light: imagine a sphere of golden light expanding from the center of your body and spreading throughout your body. This sphere of light represents your inner energy and your connection to the world.

5.   Focus on the feeling of peace: as you visualize the sphere of light, focus on the feeling of peace and tranquility that surrounds you.

6.   Focus on breathing: focus your attention on the feeling of the breath flowing through your body. Breathe deeply and slowly, trying to maintain a steady rhythm.

7.   Repeat a phrase: choose a phrase that helps you focus, such as "I am here and now" or "I am at peace and serenity." Repeat this phrase to yourself as you continue to breathe deeply.

8.   Practice meditation regularly: as with all meditation techniques, Shambala meditation requires regular practice to produce lasting results. Try to practice Shambala meditation every day, even for just a few minutes, for maximum benefits.

Shambala meditation is thus a meditation practice that can help create an inner environment of peace and calm. This practice can also be tailored to one's needs and preferences.

VIPASSIAN MEDITATION

Vipassana meditation is a Buddhist practice that focuses on mindfulness and deep understanding of the nature of the mind and the world. Vipassana meditation can help reduce stress, improve awareness and increase overall well-being.

Here is how to practice Vipassana meditation step-by-step:

1.   Choose a quiet place: choose a quiet place where you can sit comfortably without distractions or noise.
2.   Sit comfortably: sit comfortably with your back straight and your hands resting on your lap.
3.   Breathe deeply: start breathing deeply and focus on the sensation of the breath flowing through your body.
4.   Observe your mind: start observing the thoughts going through your mind without judging them or trying to change them. Simply be present and aware of your thoughts.

5.   Observe bodily sensations: focus on the bodily sensations you are experiencing at the moment, such as the sensation of the breath going in and out of your nose or the physical sensations you feel in different parts of your body.

6.   Observe emotions: observe the emotions you are experiencing at this moment, such as joy, sadness, or anger. Simply be present and aware of your emotions, without judging them or trying to change them.

7.   Observe the changing nature of things: focus your attention on the changing nature of things, observing how everything that exists is subject to change and transformation. This will help you develop a greater understanding of the true nature of reality.

8.   Practice meditation regularly: as with all meditation techniques, Vipassana meditation requires regular practice to produce lasting results. Try to practice Vipassana meditation every day, even for just a few minutes, for maximum benefits.

Vipassana meditation is a deep meditation practice that requires a fair amount of concentration and discipline. Regular practice of Vipassana meditation can help develop greater awareness of self and the world, improve relationship with self and others, and increase overall well-being.

TRANSCENDENTAL MEDITATION

Transcendental meditation is a meditation technique introduced to the West in the 1960s by Maharishi Mahesh Yogi. This practice focuses on the repetition of a specific mantra to achieve a deeper state of calm and relaxation.

Here is how to practice Transcendental meditation step-by-step:

1.   Choose a quiet place: choose a quiet place where you can sit comfortably without distractions or noise.

2.   Sit comfortably: sit comfortably with your back straight and your hands resting on your lap.

3.   Repeat the mantra: choose a specific mantra, which will be provided to you during the meditation class, and repeat it silently to yourself while breathing deeply. The mantra should be repeated naturally and not forced.

4.   Focus on the sensation of the breath: As you repeat the mantra, focus your attention on the sensation of the breath flowing through your body. Breathe deeply and slowly, trying to maintain a steady rhythm.

5.   Observe thoughts: if your thoughts stray from the mantra or breath, simply observe them and let them go. Do not judge your thoughts, but let them flow without clinging to them.

6.   Practice for 20 minutes: practice Transcendental meditation for at least 20 minutes a day, twice a day. You can gradually increase the duration of meditation up to 30 minutes.

7.   Practice regularly: as with all meditation techniques, Transcendental meditation requires regular practice to produce lasting results. Try to practice Transcendental meditation every day, even for just a few minutes, for maximum benefits.

Transcendental meditation is a meditation technique that can especially help reduce stress, improve concentration. This practice is especially suitable for those who are looking for a meditation technique that requires less effort and concentration than other techniques.

OSHO MEDITATION

Osho meditation is a meditation technique introduced by Indian philosopher and spiritual teacher Osho. This practice focuses on releasing inner energy and connecting with your deepest self.

Here is how to practice Osho meditation step-by-step:

1.   Choose a quiet place: choose a quiet place where you can sit comfortably without distractions or noise.

2.   Sit comfortably: sit comfortably with your back straight and your hands resting on your lap.

3.   Breathe deeply: start breathing deeply and focus on the sensation of the breath flowing through your body.

4.   Release your mind: relax your mind from thoughts and focus your attention on the feeling of peace and tranquility enveloping you.

5.   Experiment with various techniques: Osho came up with a wide range of meditation techniques that can be used to achieve different goals. Some of the best known techniques are Dynamic Meditation, Kundalini Meditation and No-Dimensions Meditation. Experiment with the various techniques to find the one that best suits your needs. In the following sections you will find each of these possibilities explained in more detail.

6.   Practice regularly: as with all meditation techniques, Osho meditation requires regular practice to produce lasting results. Try to practice Osho meditation every day, even if only for a few minutes, for maximum benefits.

Osho meditation is a creative and dynamic meditation practice that can help you release your inner energy and connect with your deeper self. Osho has devised a wide range of meditation techniques that can be used to achieve different goals, such as reducing stress, increasing creativity and improving mental health. With a little practice and perseverance, Osho meditation can become an important part of your daily wellness routine.

DYNAMIC MEDITATION: Dynamic Meditation is a meditation technique introduced by Osho that combines meditation with exercise and breathing. This practice can help release physical and mental tension, increase energy and improve mental health.

Here is how to practice Dynamic Meditation step-by-step:

- Choose a quiet place: choose a quiet place where you can move freely without distractions or noise.

- Follow the instructions: Dynamic Meditation is divided into five phases, each of which lasts about 10 to 15 minutes. Follow the instructions for each phase of the meditation:

- Step 1: Chaotic breathing - breathe deeply, chaotically and quickly.

- Step 2: Exhalation with shouting - exhale with a loud, powerful shout so as to release physical and mental tension.

- Step 3: Jump - jump, keeping your arms raised above your head.

- Step 4: Stop - stop jumping and stand still, silent and without thought.

- Step 5: Dance - dance freely, moving spontaneously and naturally.

Practice regularly: as with all meditation techniques, Dynamic Meditation requires regular practice to produce lasting results. Try to practice Dynamic Meditation at least once a week for maximum benefits.

Dynamic Meditation is a dynamic meditation practice that can help release physical and mental tension, increase energy and improve mental health. This practice may be particularly suitable for those who are looking for a meditation technique that combines movement and breath, and allows free expression of your emotions.

NO DYMENSIONS MEDITATION:

No-Dimensions Meditation is a meditation technique introduced by Osho that focuses on creating a limitless inner space where the mind can relax and connect with one's deeper self.

Here is how to practice No-Dimensions Meditation step-by-step:

- Choose a quiet place: choose a quiet place where you can sit comfortably without distractions or noise.

- Sit comfortably: sit comfortably with your back straight and your hands resting on your knees.

- Focus on the sensation of the breath: start by focusing on the sensation of the breath flowing through your body. Breathe deeply and slowly, trying to maintain a consistent rhythm.

- Focus on the inner light: focus your attention on the inner light shining in the center of your forehead. Imagine this light expanding, filling your entire body and creating a limitless inner space.

- Experience the endless dimension: immerse yourself in this limitless inner space, letting go of all thoughts or worries. Experience the endless dimension and the feeling of connection with your deepest self.

- Practice regularly: as with all meditation techniques, No-Dimensions Meditation requires regular practice to produce lasting results. Try to practice No-Dimensions Meditation at least once a day, even if only for a few minutes, for maximum benefits.

No-Dimensions Meditation is a meditation practice that focuses on creating a boundless inner space where the mind can relax and connect with its deeper self. This practice is particularly suitable for those seeking a meditation technique that allows them to let go of thoughts and worries, creating an inner space of peace and tranquility.

DAOIST MEDITATION

Daoist meditation is an ancient practice rooted in Daoist philosophy, based on the search for inner balance and harmony. This meditation technique focuses on the circulation of life energy, called "chi," in the body and the harmonization of yin and yang forces.

Here is how to practice Daoist meditation step-by-step:

1. Choose a quiet place: choose a quiet place where you can sit comfortably without distractions or noise.

2. Sit comfortably: sit comfortably with your back straight and your hands resting on your lap.

3. Breathe deeply: start breathing deeply and focus on the sensation of the breath flowing through your body.

4.   Focus on the center of the body: focus your attention on the center of the body, about 3 centimeters below the belly button, called the "Lower Dantian." Imagine that this area is the center of all the energy in your body.

5.   Visualize the circulation of energy: visualize energy flowing from the Lower Dantian through the body, following the path of the energy meridians. Visualize yin energy flowing upward, while yang energy flows downward, creating harmony between the two forces.

6.   Release tension: release tension in every part of the body and focus on the feeling of peace and tranquility that surrounds you.

7.   Practice regularly: as with all meditation techniques, Taoist meditation requires regular practice to produce lasting results. Try to

practice Daoist meditation every day, even for just a few minutes, for maximum benefits.

Daoist meditation is a meditation practice that focuses on the circulation of life energy in the body and the harmonization of yin and yang forces.

CHAKRA MEDITATION

Chakra meditation is a meditation practice that focuses on activating the seven main chakras, or energy cores, located along the spine. This practice can help unblock vital energy, reduce stress and increase a sense of inner balance and harmony.

Here's how to practice chakra meditation step-by-step:

1.   Choose a quiet place: choose a quiet place where you can sit comfortably without distractions or noise.

2.   Sit comfortably: sit comfortably with your back straight and your hands resting on your lap.

3.   Breathe deeply: start breathing deeply and focus on the sensation of the breath flowing through your body.

4.   Focus on the root chakra: Focus your attention on the root chakra, located at the base of the spine. Visualize a bright red circle expanding from the chakra, representing your connection to the earth.

5.   Focus on the sacral chakra: Focus your attention on the sacral chakra, located in the lower abdomen. Visualize a bright orange circle expanding from the chakra, representing your creativity and passion.

6.   Focus on the solar plexus chakra: Focus your attention on the solar plexus chakra, located in the upper abdomen. Visualize a bright yellow circle expanding from the chakra, representing your personal power.

7.   Focus on the heart chakra: Focus your attention on the heart chakra, located in the center of the chest. Visualize a bright green circle expanding from the chakra, representing love and compassion.

8.   Focus on the throat chakra: Focus your attention on the throat chakra, located in the throat. Visualize a bright blue circle expanding from the chakra, representing communication and expression.

9.   Focus on the third eye chakra: Focus your attention on the third eye chakra, located between the eyebrows. Visualize a bright purple circle expanding from the chakra, representing your intuition and subtle perception.

10.   Focus on the crown chakra: Focus your attention on the crown chakra, located at the top of the skull. Visualize a bright white circle

expanding from the chakra, representing your connection to the divine.

11. Practice regularly: as with all meditation techniques, chakra meditation requires regular practice to produce lasting results. Try to practice chakra meditation at least once a week, even if only for a few minutes, for maximum benefits.

Chakra meditation is a meditation practice that focuses on activating the seven main chakras and can help to unlock vital energy, reduce stress and increase a sense of inner balance and harmony. This practice can be useful for those who wish to develop greater awareness of their energy centers, improve their mental and physical health, and achieve greater inner balance and harmony.
In addition, chakra meditation can be customized to suit each person's individual needs. Some people may focus on one or two chakras that they feel need more work, while others may choose to focus on all seven chakras.

Like all meditation techniques, regular practice is essential to get the maximum benefits from chakra meditation. Although it may be helpful to start with a short meditation, try to set aside time each week for your practice, gradually increasing the duration of meditation.

In addition, you may find it helpful to use visualization to help you focus on individual chakras. Visualizing the color and shape of the circle representing each chakra can help you focus your mind and access the vital energy flowing through your body.

In short, chakra meditation is a powerful practice that can help you unlock vital energy and achieve greater inner balance and harmony. Experiment with this meditation technique and find the practice that works best for you.

ZEN MEDITATION

Zen meditation, or Zazen, is a form of Japanese meditation that focuses on breath awareness and reducing mental "chatter." This practice requires a rigid but relaxed posture, slow and deep breathing, and an open and focused mind.

Here is how to practice Zen meditation step-by-step:

1.   Choose a quiet place: choose a quiet place where you can sit comfortably without distractions or noise.

2.   Sit properly: sit with your back straight and legs crossed, with your hands resting on your knees. The ideal position is the lotus or half-lotus position, but you can also sit on a chair if the position on the floor is uncomfortable for you.

3.   Breathe deeply: start breathing deeply, focusing on the sensation of the breath flowing

through the body. Inhale slowly and deeply through your nose, filling your lungs with air, and then exhale slowly through your mouth.

4.   Focus on posture: Focus your attention on your posture, keeping your back straight and shoulders relaxed. Keep your gaze low, staring at the floor a few feet away, without focusing on anything in particular.

5.   Focus on breath awareness: focus your attention on breath awareness, observing the ebb and flow of breath entering and leaving your nostrils. Do not try to control the breath, but let it flow naturally.

6.   Observe your thoughts: when your thoughts wander, observe them without judgment and then return your attention to your breathing.

7. Practice regularly: as with all meditation techniques, Zen meditation requires regular practice to produce lasting results. Try to practice Zen meditation at least once a day, even if only for a few minutes, for maximum benefits.

Zen meditation is a practice that can help reduce stress, improve mental and physical health, and increase a sense of inner balance.

KUNDALINI MEDITATION

Kundalini meditation is an ancient meditation practice that focuses on activating Kundalini energy, located at the base of the spine. This practice can help release blocked energy in the body, reduce stress and increase a sense of inner balance and harmony.

Here is how to practice Kundalini meditation step-by-step:

1. Choose a quiet place: choose a quiet place where you can sit comfortably without distractions or noise.

2. Sit comfortably: sit with your back straight and legs crossed, with your hands resting on your knees.

3. Breathe deeply: start breathing deeply, focusing on the sensation of the breath flowing through your body. Inhale slowly and deeply through your nose, filling your lungs with air, and then exhale slowly through your mouth.

4. Focus on the root chakra: Focus your attention on the root chakra, located at the base of the spine. Visualize a bright red circle expanding from the chakra, representing your connection to the earth.

5. Focus on rising energy: Imagine Kundalini energy rising up the spine, passing through each main chakra. Visualize the energy as a glowing light that expands as it moves up the spine.

6. Tune into the vibration of the mantra: Use a mantra, or a series of repeated sounds or words, to help you focus and activate Kundalini energy. You can choose a specific mantra such as "Om," or use a series of sounds that create a harmonic vibration.

7.   Release blocked energy: if you feel tension or blockages in your body during meditation, breathe deeply and relax. Try to let go of the tension, releasing the blocked energy.

8.   Practice regularly: as with all meditation techniques, Kundalini meditation requires regular practice to produce lasting results. Try to practice Kundalini meditation at least once a day, even if only for a few minutes, for maximum benefits.

Kundalini meditation is a powerful practice that can help unlock vital energy, reduce stress and increase a sense of inner balance and harmony.

SAHAJA YOGA MEDITATION

Sahaja Yoga meditation is a meditation practice that focuses on balancing Kundalini energy. This practice combines elements of meditation, breathing, relaxation exercises and visualization to create a deep and highly relaxing meditation experience.

Here is how to practice Sahaja Yoga meditation step-by-step:

1.   Choose a quiet place: choose a quiet place where you can sit comfortably without distractions or noise.

2.   Sit comfortably: sit with your back straight and legs crossed, with your hands resting on your knees.

3.   Breathe deeply: start breathing deeply, focusing on the sensation of the breath flowing through your body. Inhale slowly and deeply

through your nose, filling your lungs with air, and then exhale slowly through your mouth.

4.   Activate Kundalini energy: use the power of visualization to activate Kundalini energy, imagining a stream of light moving down the spine.

5.   Focus on the coronal chakra: focus your attention on the coronal chakra, located at the top of the head. Visualize a bright white light expanding from the chakra, representing your connection to the divine.

6.   Relax and allow the flow of energy to release: breathe deeply and relax, allowing the energy to flow freely through your body.

7.   Tune into the mantra vibe: use a mantra, or a series of repeated sounds or words, to help you focus and activate your Kundalini energy.

8.   Practice regularly: as with all meditation techniques, Sahaja Yoga meditation requires regular practice to produce lasting results. Try to practice Sahaja Yoga meditation at least once a day, even if only for a few minutes, for maximum benefits.

KRIYA YOGA MEDITATION

Kriya Yoga meditation is a meditation practice that focuses on harmonizing the body's vital energy, known as prana. This practice uses a variety of breathing techniques, postures and visualizations to create a deep and highly relaxing meditation experience.

Here is how to practice Kriya Yoga meditation step-by-step:

1.   Choose a quiet place: choose a quiet place where you can sit comfortably without distractions or noise.

2.   Sit comfortably: sit with your back straight and legs crossed, with your hands resting on your knees.

3.   Breathe deeply: start breathing deeply, focusing on the sensation of the breath flowing through your body. Inhale slowly and deeply through your nose, filling your lungs with air, and then exhale slowly through your mouth.

4.   Visualize prana energy*: imagine prana energy as a bright light moving down the spine, helping to strengthen and restore balance to the nervous system.

5.   Practice breathing techniques: use a variety of breathing techniques, such as ujjayi breathing or nadi shodhana breathing (explained below), to help strengthen and harmonize prana energy.

6.   Use yoga postures: use yoga postures such as lotus or cobra pose to help unblock energy and create greater flexibility and strength in the body.

7.   Visualize the chakras: focus your attention on the seven main chakras, using visualization to

help balance and harmonize energy in each area of the body.

8.   Practice regularly: as with all meditation techniques, Kriya Yoga meditation requires regular practice to produce lasting results. Try to practice Kriya Yoga meditation at least once a day, even if only for a few minutes, for maximum benefits.

* Prana energy is a concept found in the yoga tradition and indicates the vital energy of the body. According to yogic philosophy, prana flows through subtle channels called nadis and is distributed throughout the body through the chakras, the energy centers of the body. Prana energy is considered the life force that animates and sustains life, and it is said that when the flow of prana is blocked or imbalanced, disorders and diseases occur. The practice of yoga, including breathing exercises, postures and meditation, is aimed at unblocking and harmonizing prana energy, allowing the body to function optimally

and promoting health and well-being on a physical, mental and emotional level.

UJJAYI BREATHING:

Ujjayi breathing, also known as "victorious breathing," is a yogic breathing technique that involves the contraction of the vocal cords during inhalation and exhalation. The Ujjayi breathing technique is often used during yoga practices, but it can also be practiced alone as a meditation technique.

To practice Ujjayi breathing, follow these steps:

- Sit in a comfortable position, with your spine straight and shoulders relaxed.

- Breathe normally through your nose, focusing on the sensation of the breath going in and out through your nose.

- Inhale slowly and deeply through your nose, taking the air deep into your lungs.

- Slightly contract the vocal cords, creating a sound similar to the rustling of sea waves or the sound of wind blowing through the trees.

- Exhale slowly through your nose, continuing to contract the vocal cords gently.

- Continue breathing in this way for a few minutes, focusing on the sound of your breathing and the sensation of air entering and leaving your body.

Ujjayi breathing has several benefits, including reducing stress, promoting relaxation, and improving concentration and awareness. In addition, this breathing technique can help regulate blood pressure and improve lung function. However, if you have blood pressure or breathing problems, it is recommended that you consult a doctor before practicing this breathing technique.

NADI SHODHANA BREATHING:

Nadi Shodhana breathing, also known as "alternating nostril breathing," is a yogic breathing technique that involves alternating between inhaling through one nostril and exhaling through the other, with the goal of purifying the body's energy channels and rebalancing life energy.

To practice Nadi Shodhana breathing, follow these steps:

- Sit in a comfortable position with your back straight and shoulders relaxed.

- Place your right thumb over the right nostril and slowly inhale through the left nostril.

- When you have inhaled completely, close the left nostril with the left ring finger and hold your breath for a few seconds.
- Lift your thumb from the right nostril and exhale slowly through the right nostril.

92

- Inhale through the right nostril and then, when you have inhaled fully, close the right nostril with the right thumb and hold your breath for a few seconds.

- Lift the left ring finger from the left nostril and slowly exhale through the left nostril.

- Continue breathing in this way, alternating between nostrils, for a few minutes.

Nadi Shodhana breathing is particularly useful for balancing the body's energy and promoting mental calmness. Regular practice of this breathing technique can help reduce stress, anxiety and muscle tension, as well as improve lung function and promote deep, restful sleep. However, if you have breathing problems or unstable blood pressure, consult a doctor before practicing Nadi Shodhana breathing.

TUMMO MEDITATION

Tummo meditation, also known as "inner heat meditation," is a meditation practice from Tibetan Buddhism that uses breathing and visualization to generate heat and energy in the body. This meditation technique can help reduce stress, improve health and increase awareness and concentration.

Here is how to practice Tummo meditation step-by-step:

1.   Sit comfortably: Choose a comfortable sitting position, with a straight back and crossed legs.

2.   Focus your attention on breathing: Start by breathing deeply and focusing on the sensation of the breath going in and out of your body.

3.   Visualize the internal flame: Visualize an internal flame burning in the lower abdominal area, and imagine inhaling through this flame.

4.   Practice breathing: Use a breathing technique called "fire breathing," in which you quickly inhale through your nose, contracting your abdominal muscles and generating heat.

5.   Maintain visualization of the inner flame: Keep visualizing the burning inner flame as you practice fire breathing.

6.   Relax: After a few minutes of practice, relax and continue breathing normally, focusing your attention on the feeling of heat and energy you have generated in your body.

Tummo meditation requires practice and dedication, but it can produce great health and wellness benefits. This meditation technique has been associated with reduced stress, improved immune function, and increased awareness and concentration. If you decide to practice Tummo meditation, it is important to do so under the guidance of an experienced instructor and follow instructions carefully to avoid any risks or injuries.

HANDS-ON TIPS TO IMPROVE YOUR WELL-BEING:

WHY HEALTHY EATING IS THE FIRST STEP TO A PROPER BODY-MIND BALANCE

Nutrition is a key element in mind-body well-being, and much scientific research has shown that eating healthy is the first step toward a balanced and happy life. Philosopher Feuerbach's phrase "we are what we eat" is extremely true and reflects the importance of a balanced diet for our health.

Science has now proven that a healthy, balanced diet is the first step in ensuring a balance between mind and body. In fact, many studies have shown that the nutrients in food have a direct impact on the functioning of our brain and our emotions. For example, proteins are critical for the production of neurotransmitters, such as serotonin, that affect our mood and state of mind. Similarly, omega-3 fatty acids are known for their role in brain health and their ability to reduce stress and anxiety.

Therefore, a poor diet can have negative effects on concentration, stress, and anxiety. For example, a diet high in sugar and processed foods can increase inflammation levels in the body, cause blood sugar spikes, and alter brain functioning. In addition, a lack of essential nutrients, such as B vitamins, can lead to reduced concentration and memory.

To fully enjoy the benefits of good nutrition, it is important not only to choose the right foods, but also to pay attention to how you eat them. Drinking and eating slowly, enjoying mealtimes, and maintaining an proper level of hydration all help to ensure good concentration and reduce stress.

Healthy eating is also important for concentration and memory. According to some studies, eating foods high in fat and sugar can increase the likelihood of suffering from long-term memory and concentration problems. In contrast, a balanced diet rich in essential nutrients, such as fruits and vegetables, can increase the ability to concentrate and improve memory.

In addition, poor nutrition can also increase stress and anxiety levels. For example, eating too many foods high in sugar and fat can cause energy spikes but, subsequently, a drastic drop in energy. This can lead to feelings of fatigue and irritability, which can increase stress and anxiety levels. In contrast, a healthy, balanced diet can help maintain stable energy levels and improve mental and physical well-being.

In conclusion, diet has a significant impact on our bodies and minds. It is important to take time for each meal, drink plenty of water and eat well and slowly to get the most out of your diet and to prevent problems with concentration, stress and anxiety.

DAILY GRATITUDE, THE VALUE OF PRACTICING GRATITUDE

The art of gratitude is one of the most important practices for psychological well-being and life in general. Gratitude helps us recognize the privileges we often take for granted and focus on what we have instead of what we lack. Practicing gratitude daily can have a significant positive impact on our lives, helping us develop a more optimistic outlook, increase our sense of contentment and happiness, and reduce negativity.

A simple practice for developing gratitude is to write daily sentences for what you have and appreciate about life. This can be done in a personal journal, in a notebook or even on your phone, and consists of writing down what you are grateful for each day. One can write small things, such as a beautiful sunset, a good day at work, a hot cup of coffee, a sunny day... For example, one can write "I am thankful for my job that allows me to earn money," "I am thankful for my friends who always support me," or "I am thankful for my health that allows me to live a busy life."

In addition to writing, it is also important to become aware of what you are grateful for throughout the day. For example, taking a moment to acknowledge what we have during meals or before bed can help develop a positive mindset. Also, trying to focus on the present and the best moments instead of the past or future can help develop gratitude.

Moreover, practicing gratitude not only affects our inner perception, but also has a positive impact on our relationships with others. In fact, another way to practice gratitude is to express it toward others. Thanking someone for what they have done or what they are can increase the sense of connection and well-being for both parties.

In conclusion, being grateful on a daily basis for what we have or experience is a powerful practice that allows us to cultivate a positive attitude and to create healthier and more meaningful relationships with others helping us to be more satisfied and fulfilled.

WRITING A PERSONAL JOURNAL

Writing a personal journal can be a very useful and beneficial activity for one's mind and well-being. Many scientific studies have shown that regularly writing down one's thoughts and emotions can have many positive benefits on mental and psychological well-being.

First, writing a personal journal allows us to clear our minds of the worries and negative emotions that we often accumulate throughout the day. When we write down our thoughts, we can see them on the page and analyze them more objectively, separating ourselves from the emotions that accompany them. This process helps us process and manage our thoughts and emotions more effectively, reducing stress and anxiety.

In addition, writing a personal journal helps us recognize our recurring thoughts and negative emotions, which often prevent us from seeing life from a more positive perspective.

By writing down our thoughts regularly, we can become aware of our fears and negative thought patterns, and then take control of the situation and change them.

Writing a personal journal also helps us express our gratitude for the good and positive things in our lives. When we write down the things we are grateful for, we can focus on the blessings and opportunities present in our lives, instead of focusing on what is missing or causing us pain. This helps us develop a more positive and optimistic attitude toward life.

In addition to the traditional journal in which one generally writes a summary of the day with the emotions felt during events, there are also other types of personal journals that can be useful for expressing one's thoughts and emotions. One example is a poetry diary, in which one can write verses describing our emotions and thoughts. This type of diary is especially useful for those who have poetic talent or who want to express their thoughts in a more creative way.

Another type of personal journal that can be kept is an outlet journal, where one can write down thoughts and emotions that plague us or cause us stress. This type of journal can be used as a way to clear the mind and process thoughts and emotions that can be difficult to deal with.

In addition, there are also journals that can be kept for specific purposes, such as a gratitude journal in which we write down the things we are grateful for each day, or a meditation journal in which we write down our reflections and experiences during meditation practice.

Either way, the important thing is to find the type of journal that best suits one's needs and allows us to express our thoughts and emotions in an effective and satisfying way.

Writing a personal journal is a very useful activity for mental health and personal well-being, and should be considered a habit to include in one's daily routine; in fact, it provides us with a solid foundation for personal growth and development. When we regularly write down our thoughts and emotions, we can see the progress we have made over time, and we can recognize patterns of thinking and behavior that prevent us from growing and developing.

In summary, writing a personal journal can be a very useful and beneficial activity for our mind and well-being. Not only it helps us process and manage our thoughts and emotions, but it also helps us develop a more positive attitude.

THE VALUE OF READING IN MENTAL WELL-BEING

Reading is an activity that has great beneficial power for mental well-being. Many scientific studies have shown that reading has the power to increase the volume of gray matter in the brain, meaning that people who read regularly have greater cognitive capacity than those who do not. Reading also helps us cultivate critical thinking, increasing our ability to understand and analyze the world around us.

In addition, reading has the power to increase intelligence and creativity, as well as positively affect our thought patterns. When we read a book, we are able to immerse ourselves in new experiences, see the world through other people's eyes, and gain knowledge that could be invaluable to us. In this way, reading becomes a powerful tool for expanding our understanding of the world and enriching our inner life.

Reading also offers us an escape from reality, giving us a chance to escape from our daily problems and immerse ourselves in fantastic, imaginary worlds. This can help reduce stress and anxiety, allowing us to relax and feel calmer and more invigorated. In addition, reading allows us to develop empathy and understanding toward others, helping us to put ourselves in others' shoes and understand their emotions and thoughts.

In summary, reading is an activity that can have a very positive impact on our mental health, enriching our lives and helping us become more intelligent, creative and sensitive people. It is important to devote time to reading, whether books, newspapers, magazines or online articles, to take full advantage of its positive effects.

THE IMPORTANCE OF CONTACT WITH NATURE

Nature is an unlimited source of mental and physical well-being. Scientific studies have shown that spending time outdoors and immersed in nature has positive effects on mental and physical health. Being immersed in nature, whether it is a walk in the mountains or a picnic in the park, helps us recharge our batteries and relax, thereby increasing our quality of life. In addition, being surrounded by the beauty of nature, with its colors, scents and sounds, helps us to focus and relax, moving away from daily stress.

In addition, contact with nature also has a positive impact on the nervous and immune systems. Nature helps us reduce levels of anxiety and depression by promoting the production of endorphins and serotonin, neurotransmitters responsible for feelings of well-being and happiness. In addition, walking outdoors and surrounded by nature improves memory and concentration, and has a positive effect on physical health, helping us maintain a good balance between mind and body.

Finally, nature is a source of inspiration and creativity. Being immersed in the beauty and peace of nature helps us clear our minds and focus on the important things in life, giving us the opportunity for reflection and increased creativity. In addition, nature helps us develop greater awareness and a sense of gratitude for all that we have, and teaches us the importance of caring for the environment and the world around us.

In addition, exposure to sunlight is a very important aspect of mental well-being. Sunlight helps us regulate our circadian rhythm, increase levels of serotonin (the feel-good hormone) and reduce levels of melatonin (the hormone that makes us feel tired). This allows us to have a more restful sleep and wake up more refreshed. In addition, exposure to sunlight helps prevent seasonal depression and improve our mood and overall energy.

Furthermore, scientific research has shown that exposure to sunlight can also help prevent chronic diseases such as osteoporosis and depression. Sunlight also provides us with vitamin D, which is important for bone health and the immune system.

It is important to note that exposure to sunlight should not be excessive, because too much exposure can cause sunburn and skin damage. It is important to try to expose ourselves to sunlight during the early hours of the day, when UV radiation levels are lowest, and to protect the skin with sunscreen and appropriate clothing.

In conclusion, contact with nature is a key element for mental and physical well-being. Spending time outdoors and immersed in the beauty of nature helps us relax, increase concentration and memory, improve physical health, and increase creativity and awareness. Therefore, do not hesitate to take a moment each day to enjoy the benefits of nature and rediscover the peace and well-being it can offer us.

THE IMPORTANCE OF PHYSICAL ACTIVITY

Physical activity is a key element in mental well-being. The Roman poet Juvenal said "mens sana in corpore sana" (literally: "a healthy mind in a healthy body"), a phrase placed to emphasize the absolute importance of having a balance between physical and mental well-being.

Exercise has a positive effect on mental health and can help prevent depression, anxiety and stress. Exercise, in addition, increases the production of endorphins, chemicals that improve mood and help reduce stress. In addition, physical activity can increase self-esteem and self-confidence, promoting a greater sense of well-being and happiness.

In addition, exercise has a positive effect on brain function and helps improve memory and concentration. Regular exercise has been associated with increased brain plasticity, meaning that the brain is better able to adapt and respond to cognitive challenges. This can be especially helpful in preventing and managing conditions such as depression, anxiety, and age-related cognitive decline.

Physical activity is a great way to release tension and energy built up throughout the day. It can help reduce stress and clear the mind, allowing a person to focus better and be more productive. In addition, it can also be a great way to socialize and form positive relationships with others, further improving mental well-being.

To sum up, physical activity is an important part of a healthy lifestyle and can have a positive effect on mental well-being. It is important that people find a type of physical activity that they enjoy and that can be easily integrated into their daily routine. This can include walking, jogging, going to the gym, or playing a team sport. The important thing is that the activity chosen is regular and allows the person to be able to relieve themselves from accumulated tension.

EXPOSE THE MIND TO CREATIVE INPUT

The importance of exposing the mind to creative stimulation has been amply demonstrated by much scientific research. Creativity is a key component of mental well-being, and subjecting one's mind to creative stimulation is one way to keep it fit and increase one's happiness and productivity. Here are 10 daily activities that can help stimulate the mind's creativity:

1.   Grow a garden or take care of plants at home. Nature is a great source of inspiration, and cultivating the earth and taking care of plants is a way to get in touch with it and unleash your creativity.

2.   Do a puzzle or play a board game. These activities are a way to test one's logic and problem-solving skills, and they can be very stimulating for the mind.

3.   Learn a new skill or hobby. Experimenting with new things and learning new skills is a great way to stimulate creativity and keep the mind young and flexible.

4.   Write a journal or blog. Writing is a great way to express your thoughts and emotions, and it can help stimulate creativity and explore new ideas.

5.   Reading books or watching movies. These activities can help cultivate one's imagination and explore new ideas and perspectives.

6.   Traveling or visiting new places. Traveling and discovering new places can be very inspiring and help stimulate creativity.

7.   Making music or singing. Music is a powerful art that can help stimulate creativity and imagination.

8.   Drawing or painting. These art activities are a great way to express yourself and stimulate your creativity.

9.   Practice meditation or yoga. These practices can help you relax your mind and release your creativity.

10. Spend time with friends and family. Spending time with loved ones can be very inspiring and can help stimulate creativity.

In addition, creating art is a great way to stimulate creativity. You could, indeed, engage in a creative hobby such as painting, sculpting, photography or creating music. Creating something beautiful and meaningful will help you free your mind and express your emotions in a creative and positive way. Writing can also be a very powerful creative activity. Writing a short story, a poem or, as we said, a journal can help you explore your thoughts and emotions in a creative way.

Problem solving can also be a form of creativity. Facing challenges and solving problems requires thinking outside the box and seeing things from different perspectives. This helps to develop creativity and keep the mind active and exercised.

Finally, meditation and yoga practice are great ways to stimulate creativity. Meditation helps calm the mind and focus on the present, while yoga encourages physical and mental flexibility. Both of these practices can help reduce stress and clear the mind, creating an ideal environment for creativity.

In conclusion, subjecting your mind to creative stimulation is very important for mental and physical well-being. It allows you to explore your thoughts and emotions creatively, free your mind from stress, and keep your mind active and exercised. So, choose a creative activity that you enjoy and devote yourself to it daily to take full advantage of its potential.

LEARNING TO FIND OUR OWN PERSONAL SLEEP CYCLE

The circadian cycle is a biological process that regulates our body's daily activities, such as sleeping and waking. Each of us has our own unique circadian rhythm, which can be influenced by various factors, such as genetics, age, environment, and habits. Understanding and respecting one's circadian cycle is crucial for mental well-being.

Finding one's balance and respecting it can also have a great impact on our productivity. Following a regular sleep cycle appropriate to one's needs can help prevent fatigue and improve concentration and long-term memory

People who wake up early in the morning and are productive and active during the day are known as "early birds." On the other hand, people who prefer to sleep longer and are more active at night are referred to as "night owls." It is important to understand that there is no right or wrong way to be, but that each of us has our own unique biological rhythm that is important to respect.

One way to follow one's circadian cycle is to figure out how many hours of sleep one needs. Most people need an average of 7 to 9 hours of sleep per night, but some people may need more or less time. It is important to find your own balance and follow it.

In addition, meeting your needs also means maintaining a regular sleep routine. Trying to go to bed and wake up at the same time every day helps the body regulate its biological rhythm and increase productivity during the day.

Light is also an important factor in keeping to one's circadian cycle. Daylight helps maintain wakefulness, and artificial light at night can interfere with sleep. It is important to try to limit exposure to artificial light before bedtime and take advantage of daylight when you are awake to help your body maintain its biological rhythm.

In summary, understanding and respecting one's circadian cycle is important for productivity and mental well-being. Maintaining a regular sleep routine, limiting exposure to artificial light at night, and taking advantage of daylight are ways to help the body regulate its biological rhythm.

HOW TO USE CAFFEINE TO YOUR ADVANTAGE WITHOUT ABUSING IT

Caffeine is a naturally occurring stimulant found in many foods and beverages, such as coffee, tea, chocolate, and some energy drinks. Caffeine has been shown to help improve concentration, energy, and mental performance, but it is important to note that too much caffeine can have negative effects on physical and mental well-being. The negative effects of caffeine can include insomnia, nervousness, increased blood pressure, anxiety, and addiction.

To make the most of the benefits of caffeine while avoiding the negative effects, it is important to adopt a healthy and balanced strategy. Here are some tips that can help:

• Know your tolerance: The amount of caffeine everyone can tolerate varies depending on several factors such as weight, age, and general health. It is important to understand what is the ideal amount of caffeine for you.

- Drink in moderation: The recommended amount of caffeine per day is about 400 milligrams, or about four cups of coffee. It is important not to overdo it and to limit caffeine intake, especially in the evening hours to avoid interfering with sleep.

- Choose healthy sources of caffeine: Instead of opting for energy drinks that often contain large amounts of sugar and empty calories, choose healthy sources of caffeine such as coffee or green tea.

- Take advantage of energy spikes: Caffeine enters the bloodstream within about 30 minutes of intake and reaches peak concentration within an hour and a half. Use this time for activities that require concentration or energy, such as studying or exercise.

- Maintain a balance: It is important to balance caffeine intake with other natural energy sources such as a balanced diet, regular exercise, and a healthy sleep routine.

By following these tips, you can leverage the benefits of caffeine in a healthy and strategic way. Caffeine can be an important ally in improving concentration and mental performance, but it is a weapon that should be used sparingly and wisely.

CONCENTRATION TECHNIQUES

Concentration techniques are used in many meditative, yoga, and breathing practices to help develop and improve the ability to focus the mind and maintain attention. The ability to concentrate can be useful in many situations, from daily life to sports performance, from work to study. There are many concentration techniques available, and the choice of a technique will often depend on an individual's personal preferences and specific goals.

One of the most common concentration techniques is breath concentration. In this technique, one focuses on the sensation of the breath entering and leaving the nostrils. When the mind becomes distracted, one simply returns to focusing on the breath. This concentration technique is very simple and can be practiced anywhere, anytime.

Another common concentration technique is focusing on an object. One focuses on the object, such as a candle or a statue, and tries to maintain concentration on that object for a period of time. This technique can help develop the ability to focus your attention and improve awareness.

Visualization is another common concentration technique. In this technique, one focuses on a mental image, such as a landscape or object, and tries to visualize it clearly in the mind. This technique can be useful for developing imagination and visualization skills, which can be useful in many activities, such as sports or artistic creation.

Mantra meditation is another widely used concentration technique. In this technique, one focuses on a continuously repeated word or phrase known as a mantra. Repetition of the mantra can help clear the mind of other thoughts and improve the ability to concentrate.

Finally, the mindfulness technique is another popular concentration technique. In this technique, attention is paid to the present moment, without judging or reacting to thoughts or emotions. The practice of mindfulness can help develop the ability to concentrate and be mindful, which can be useful in many situations in daily life.

In addition, here are 10 practical tips that can be applied with simple moves to increase concentration in daily life:

1.   Take breaks: Take regular breaks during work or study to relax your mind and body and prevent mental fatigue.

2.   Organize your work space: Keep your work space clean and tidy, removing all distractions.

3.   Set clear goals: Set specific and realistic goals for your work or study and focus on them.

4.   Use planning techniques: Use planning techniques, such as to-do lists or calendars, to organize your tasks and keep them under control.

5.   Reduce distractions: Get rid of distractions, such as background noise, notifications on your smartphone or e-mail messages, to better focus on your work.

6.   Maintain a healthy lifestyle: Maintain a healthy lifestyle, with a balanced diet, regular exercise and proper rest, to keep your mind and body healthy.

7.   Be aware of your work rhythm: Be aware of your work rhythm and the time of day when you are most productive. Plan your activities according to this rhythm to maximize your productivity.

8.   Practice meditation: Meditation can help improve concentration and awareness, so try incorporating a short meditation session into your daily routine.

9.   Do one thing at a time: Focus on one thing at a time, avoiding multitasking and distracting yourself from multiple tasks at once.

10.   Be motivated: Keep your motivation up by visualizing your goals, celebrating your successes and remembering why you are doing what you are doing. Motivation can be a great boost to increase focus and productivity.

DOPAMINE DETOX

Dopamine detox, or dopamine detoxification, is a practice that has gained popularity in recent years as a way to cleanse the brain of excessive overstimulation. The theory behind this practice is that constant exposure to rewarding stimuli, such as social media, junk food, gambling, pornography, drugs, excessive work and other dopamine-intensive behaviors, can lead to a decrease in the brain's sensitivity to dopamine and its inability to experience pleasure from normal, healthy activities.

Dopamine is a neurotransmitter produced by the brain in response to pleasurable and rewarding input, and its main function is to motivate people to seek pleasure and reward. However, overstimulation of this neurotransmitter can lead to decreased dopamine receptor sensitivity and decreased pleasure and satisfaction in normal activities. This is the concept behind the practice of dopamine detox.

Dopamine detox consists of a day or period of time in which one disconnects from pleasurable stimuli high in dopamine, such as television, social media, technology, junk food, alcohol, and other drugs. The goal is to eliminate these distractions for a short period of time to cleanse the brain of excessive overstimulation and restore receptor sensitivity.

The practice of dopamine detox can help reduce dependence on pleasurable stimuli high in dopamine and restore thereby increasing motivation and the ability to experience pleasure and satisfaction from normal, everyday activities. In addition, it can help reduce stress, increase productivity, and improve sleep quality. To practice dopamine detox, it is recommended to choose a day or period of time when you can devote yourself completely to the practice. During this period, completely remove all high dopamine triggers, including social media, television, junk food, drugs, alcohol, and other similar stimuli. Instead, engage in activities that do not stimulate dopamine, such as meditation, reading, gardening or yoga. The practice of dopamine detox should not be used as a substitute for medical therapy or treatment, but rather as a self-improvement technique. It is important to consult a doctor or specialist before beginning any new practice.

CONCLUSION

In conclusion, meditation and mindfulness can have a significant impact on our lives. Not only can these practices help us reduce stress and anxiety, but they can also increase our awareness and sense of presence in the present moment. Meditation and mindfulness teach us to be more aware of our emotions, thoughts and actions, and allow us to develop a sense of compassion and kindness toward ourselves and others. These benefits can help improve our relationship with ourselves and other people, increasing our happiness and sense of satisfaction in life. Meditation and mindfulness require constant practice and dedication, but their results can be significant. With practice, we can learn to stay in the present moment, find inner peace and develop a calmer, more peaceful mind.

Thank you for reading this book, I hope you enjoyed it and that it can help you in your spiritual journey.

If you think you enjoyed this book and it helped you, I only ask you to take a few seconds to leave a short review on the platform where you purchased it!

Thank you,

Yumi Tanaka

Printed in Great Britain
by Amazon